Four Funny Potatoes!

Words & Pictures by:
Len Foley

Hi Taylore
Len Foley

Dedicated to my niece River, who for some unknown reason, believes her Uncle Lenny is a potato.

Action!!!

Text © 2018 Len Foley
Pictures © 2018 Len Foley
Cover and internal design © 2018 Len Foley

All rights reserved. No part of this book may be reproduced or transmitted in any form or by any means whatsoever without express written permission from the author, except in the case of brief quotations embodied in critical articles and reviews. Please refer all pertinent questions to the publisher.

Special thanks to Rebecca (my wife) who thankfully made me change the ending and Skyler Colangelo for her careful and insightful suggestions that made the book better every week. Also to my daughter Sofia who learned the potato rhymes by heart and recited them to me daily until the book was done. And to Kat Mottram, Michelle Clarke, Brooke Sliger, Donnie G. on the Backup, Judy Gauthier and Eric Foley for their helpful suggestions and support.

Published by:

New Horizon Health, Inc.
Westlake Village, CA 91362

ISBN: 978-0-692-06978-3

Eenie... Meenie... Miney... Mo?

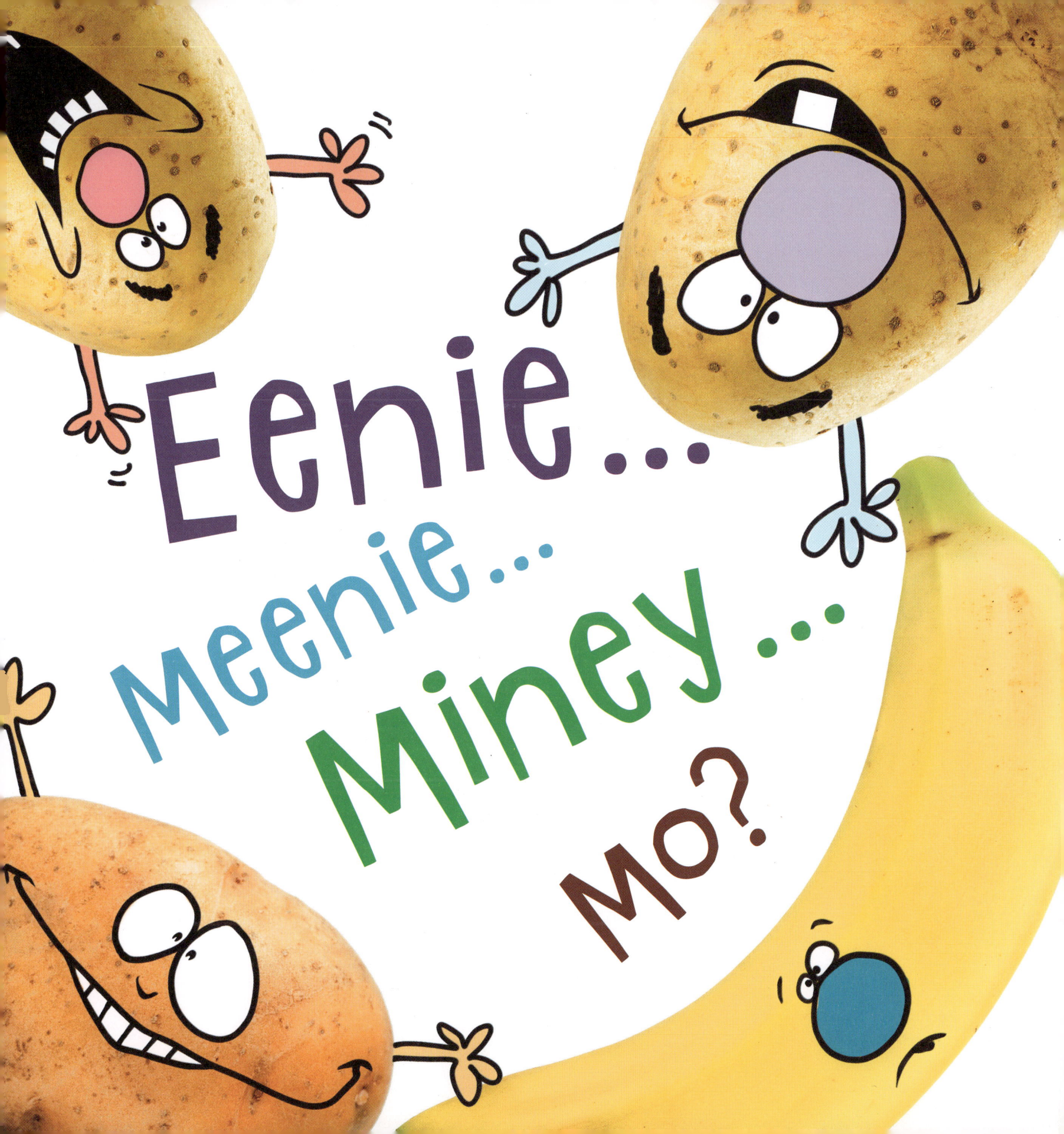

We are the four funny
PO-TA-TOES

During the Day we SLEEP in our Bowl

But at night we jump out and put on a SHOW!

This is Arnie who knows how to **dance.**

And good ol' Jimmy who wears funny **pants.**

Check out Marvin who juggles tomatoes.

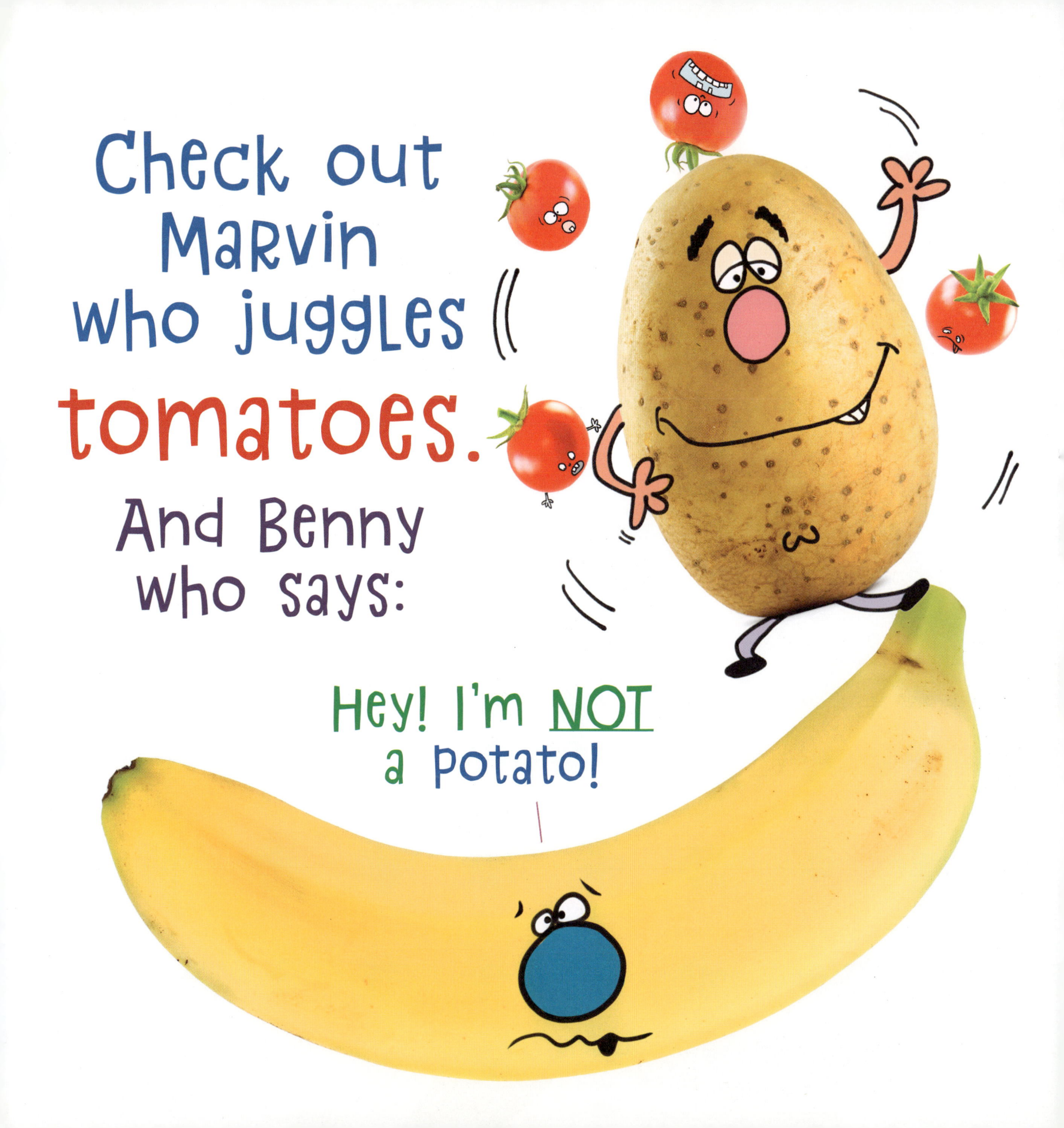

And Benny who says:

Hey! I'm NOT a potato!

Sofia the sandwich stands on one hand.

While the two silly Egg Heads sing songs in a pan.

The Goofy Grape Brothers do Back Flips off a chair...

While Jesse the Jelly Bean tosses a <u>watermelon</u> in the air!

But the real show starts when the potatoes Link arms

And sing in perfect harmony their favorite potato song...

♪ One potato, ♪♪
two potato,
three potato... ♪

NO!!

I told you guys I'm <u>not</u> a potato, so I can't be in your show.

CUT!! CUT!! Stop the rehearsal!

Benny! You are messing up your lines!

The song goes:
One potato, two potato, three potato...
FOUR!

We're the funny potatoes who could ask for more?

How many times do I need to **SAY??** I am not a potato in *any* **way!!**

I am **long and skinny,** not PUDGY and ROUND...

My body is **Shiny** and **YELLOW** not LUMPY and **BROWN.**

I have a green tip on my head not a round cap under my beanie

So that makes me...

A **YELLOW** zucchini?

No! I am a banana!!

And I am <u>one</u> of a kind.

I have my own shape,
my own color,
my own thoughts,
my own mind.

I am proud to be a banana.

I am proud to sing MY songs.

But most of all I love to sing when <u>others</u> sing along.

A lovely **Banana!**

Yes, finally! Someone sees me for who I am!

Let's sing <u>my</u> song, gang!

As LOUD as we can!

One Banana...
Two Banana...
Donuts...
...and some fries!

Three Banana...
Four Banana...
A peanut...
...and a pie!

Five
Banana...
Six
Banana...

A meatball...

...And a
Bean.

We all sing *best* when we're singing as a team!

I love yummy Bananas!

HEY!

Run for your lives!

I can't run! I don't have any feet!

Then maybe you should ROLL!!

Aw, man!

Chomp! Chomp! Chomp!

R.I.P.
Benny

Beloved
Potato

How many times do I need to say? I am not a potato in any way!

Photo by Michael Roud

Len Foley spent most of his life as a horrible writer. He wrote and self-published seven badly-written books that nobody wanted to read. And then his daughter Sofia was born and he started telling her funny rhymes and drawing pictures that made her laugh and giggle.

And that's when Len realized he wasn't a bad writer... he was writing the wrong kinds of books!

Nowadays, you won't find Len trying to write the Great American Novel, but you will find him making up stories about potatoes and smelly socks.

Check out Len's other book: Sigfried's Smelly Socks! Available on Amazon.com